Vile Lilt

Vile Lilt

Nada Gordon

ROOF BOOKS
NEW YORK

ISBN 078-1-931824-49-1

Library of Congress Control Number: 2013931835

Author photo by Spencer Lloyd. Cover and book design by Nada Gordon.
Cover photo by Linda Olsavsky. Proofreading by Jordan Davis.

Versions, possibly unrecognizable, of these pieces have appeared in
magazines such as *POETRY, Eoagh,* and *OCHO,* and on blogs such as Sina
Queyras' lemonhound.blogspot.com, and my own ululate.blogspot.com. I am
almost certain that versions have appeared elsewhere as well, and regret
any inadvertent omission. "Poetry is Junk" was composed for the panel
"Conceptual Writings" at the Advancing Feminist Poetics conference in New
York City in 2009. "Uzumaki" and "Navrang" in the second section of the
book are scripts for "neo-benshi" (live film narration) performances I gave
between 2007 and 2010. "Opaque Birds a la Wunderkammer" appeared as
part of Suzanne Bocanegra's recipe card project. "Beatles' Ex-Wives Reunion"
was performed at the Medicine Show in 2011.

To so very many: deep thanks and love for helping me through.

Roof books are distributed by
Small Press Distribution
1341 Seventh Street
Berkeley, CA 94710-1403
Phone orders: 800-869-7553
spdbooks.org

State of the Arts

NYSCA

This book was made possible, in part, with public funds
from the New York State Council on the Arts, a state agency.

ROOF BOOKS are published by
Segue Foundation
300 Bowery
New York, NY 10012
seguefoundation.com

for Claude

Nada's Garden of Versus

Fanciful Things

Sorrow

It's just my wish to, my satisfaction in, in, in gloating, the fa—
gloating. Just gloating. The poetry is gloating. It's not getting
up things, fanciful things. I had no business to mention fay and
elf in it. I seem, I always feel sorry about that. But the, that's,
uh, the, to the,

~Robert Frost

NADA'S
GARDEN OF
VERSUS

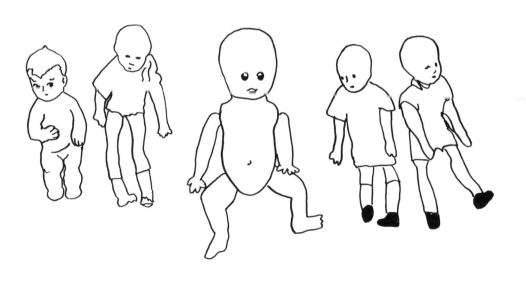

Poetry is Junk

I can tolerate the ornaments of the Kaffir, the Persian, the Slovak
peasant woman, my shoemaker's ornament, for they all have no
other way of attaining the high point of their existence. We have
art, which has taken the place of "ornament."

~Adolf Loos, Ornament and Crime

Wear your costumes with conviction—by which
we mean decide what picture you will make of yourself,
make it and then enjoy it! It is only by letting
your personality animate your costume
that you make yourself superior to the lay figure
or the sawdust doll. Swathe it in clouds of fake smoke,
snake oil, blue taupe silk, a tangle of vines.
I hover as a fever, I serve as a hot welt. The magma's
gruesome: its cardinal fierceness rumbles in
the public spaces of my prattling verse. Personality
carries great responsibilities, because we expect it to represent us
as individuals. We should therefore clothe our personality
with ballooning finery and papery ruffled taffeta interrogations;
how else to perform the burgeoning imperatives of my (our)
pandoral catachreses? A large placenta emerges
smelling of maple and bluejays. Poetry is junk.
I ache out the law of soaring, my human brain dividing
the spoils, describing a lacy arabesque on ice until
something just breaks. The ear of a woman is usually
clear pink, not ill-shaped, and there is a note of
individuality about it, the attractiveness of which
one should emphasize, not conceal. I want all of you
here with me. Hi! Hi everybody! Femmage.
I'm here as a passionate dunce, still skating the well-

worn arabesque, sincere as butter but twice as musical.
Look, this is a zither of affect: its octaves are multiplied
by the vocabulary of others, and if I feel it more intensely
then so will you. The beautiful girl inserts the dildo
and turns it around, shivering in pleasure. It gets covered
with her secretions: primal cream. The writing is the dildo,
and the girl, and the secretions. It's like learning other languages.
Vocabularies expand infinitely, tourmaline glitters in a damp cave.
Rob Fitterman writes, "I am interested
in the inclusion of subjectivity and personal
experience; I just prefer if it isn't my own. "Own?"
Expression irrigates expression. Me and the multitudes
form a lacy network: no containment, just connections: me
and the multitudes weave into each other. Drew
Gardner: "Your own handwriting is collective."
Who's containable? I'm all apertures.
Dana Ward: "Correlated ooh la las between us."
No one's not a sieve: desire leaks: we drool
when screen lovers kiss. It's all language, antic
and lascivious. Susana Gardner posts an update
quoting Mina Loy: "LOVE of others is
the appreciation of one's self. MAY your egotism
be so gigantic that you comprise mankind
in your self-sympathy." I steal with love and
out of sympathy. Both love and poetry are
alien visitations here in the breathable
room of lazy heresies, and I am writing this for you
(the primordial you) (the resonating body)
with my weeping heart and ornamental personality.
Aesthetic intimacy—not distance—but not for "authenticity."
Behold the fruits de mer of this torrid cornucopia: the sea belt,
the furbelows, the dabberlocks, the sea lace. Proper regard
for the "intimate little feminine things"—that is the secret

of charming individuality. Gathered rosebuds, re-strewn.
Gaudy miasma of decoration. If decorative woman
makes up her mind to retain a line or limit, she does it,
but only because she wants to, and not because you told her to.
This can be demonstrated by the use of silver stockings
or magenta slippers with magenta stockings.
Licking the wounds of love in four-inch platforms.
Since all words are already concepts, I'm giddy with concepts.
Let's call instead, with Lippard and Chandler, this thing we do,
ultra-conceptual. That sounds better, like dish soap.
Here I am wandering in lupine, and Queen Anne's
lace, and mariposa lilies, and wild irises, and because
they are beautiful (and grotesque, like all flowers)
they compel me and I steal them and arrange them,
Flowers are nature's readymades. The words of "others"
are warm salt blossoms. I run a mermaid ranch in my
eerie birth canal, and this aeronautic palaver is a saucy pose.
Listen. Some people hold the mistaken idea that ornament
is all very well perhaps for those who like it, but that what
they want is something practical. A pot roast of unicorn,
perhaps? Or braised mermaids? The works of Nature
gently rebuke this cold utilitarian spirit, and afford us countless
illustrations of beauty wedded to use. The painting of the petals
of the commonest wayside weed, the exquisite markings
on shells so minute that only the microscope enables us
to appreciate their beauty, the gorgeous colouring of the peacock's
feathers, the rich markings on the wings of the butterfly,
the splendour of colour of the ruby and topaz, the graceful forms
of the evanescent snow crystals, are but a few instances
that at once rise to our minds. This is the horn section
of my cavernous malady, its logical loops and mathematic
baobobs. Baobobs. Under the baobobs and mooning.
A woman is prettier when she is sensitive. She must be taught

not to throw away her honey. Honey and salt soak into
the shuddering lace. One who has never made lace—
that is—the bobbin variety—cannot imagine the charm
of the softly clinking, tinkling bobbins, like the singing of
a simmering teakettle, or like a lullaby gently hummed
in the twilight. I see Guy and Kathy and Yoko and Lucy
in the spermy sky with fighter planes, hanabi, a zillion
idiolects, and legions of anonymous females. Their DNA sings.
Their merry little jingle is very soothing, and some physicians
claim that the rhythmic effect is most beneficial to the nerves.
Doubtless, the regular shifting of the bobbins—keeping the mind,
eyes and fingers busy, proves a means of working
off overwrought feelings and serves the same quieting purpose
that piano-playing does for some tensely strung nerves.
Our nerves preserve us from isolation: I skate on my nervous
arabesque. The bad surplus smiles at the lonely preeners,
and stinky sculptures spring up where there were none
before, and that's kinda cool in the prosodic tinniness
of this cranial bhangra, you know, I love
my dog I don't have a dog, I love the paper clock
that threatens sudden endings, I love the conversations
that play air guitar in my genetic memories.
One well-known sanitarium has, with such an end in view,
introduced bobbin-lace making, and whether or not it is directly
calming the patients' jangled nerves, it is doing so indirectly,
by taking their thoughts off themselves and absorbing
their interest in seeing grow under their very fingers
so pixy a product. Woman, the instrument of reproduction,
pours into life's cauldron the best of herself, unstinted,
unmeasured, singing: "Boys, eat a plastic peach for me
in the flawed wisdom of your stretchy
genitalia, and I will sing a hurting song for you
while the peevish she-crabs wail." Lace-making

is one of those pursuits which, seeming tedious
to the onlooker, have an undeniable
fascination for the maker; and it seems as though
almost no one who really enters upon its enticing
pathway ever cares to turn back. That's because
every molecule remembers a time before time,
and if I open up to receive all emotional messages (for example,
in my food), it's because that's the kind of maladroit
I am: preponed, animated, reticular, birdish. Mawkish.
Girlish! All conceptuality in writing is feminine because it is
aware of itself being looked at. One may follow
Woman Decorative in the Orient on vase, fan, screen
and kakemono; as she struts in the stiff manner of Egyptian
bas reliefs, across walls of ancient ruins, or sits in angular serenity,
gazing into the future through the narrow slits of Egyptian eyes,
oblivious of time; woman, beautiful in the European sense,
and decorative to the superlative degree, on Greek vase
and sculptured wall. All writing is crafty, rhetorical, sited,
intertextual, posed. Here in rhythmic curves,
she dandles lovely Cupid on her toe; serves as vestal virgin
at a woodland shrine; wears the bronze helmet of Minerva; makes
laws, or as Penelope, the wife, wearily awaits her roving lord.
I feed off everything, especially my own haunted breasts.
My thoughts, my verse, my size, my clothes.
She moves in august majesty, a sore-tried queen,
and leaps in merry laughter as a care-free slave; pipes,
sings and plies the distaff. Can one possibly escape
our theme—Woman as Decoration? This milky force
of cerebration? No, for she is carved in wood and stone;
as Mother of Gawd and Queen of Electric Ladyland
she gleams in the jeweled windows of the monitor, looks down
in placid serenity on lighted altar; is woven into Gracie Allen,
in fact dominates all art, panting, slinky or marvelous,

throughout the gleaming monstrosity of the ages.
Knowing all there is to know of my subjectivity,
which is also yours, and everyone's, I have had the genius
to weave the innumerable and perplexing threads
into a tapestry of words, where the main ideas
take their places in the foreground, standing
in futile contradistinction to the deftly woven,
unintelligible and obtruding background.
My underpants have their own ideas.
The meaning shifts pleasurably.
I always confuse "midrash" and "midriff."
One sets out gaily to study costumes, full
of the courage of ignorance, the joyous optimism
of an enthusiast, because it is amusing and looks
so simple with all the material, old and new,
lying about one. My fingers summon it with little clicks,
caressing information. Hollow noise pools up in my candy
head. Frenetic clutch. Noxious erudite
suggestiveness. I babble and I am sticky with live cultures.
Women whose throats are getting lined should
take to jeweled dog-collars, and skirts of black tulle
or net, caught up with great rhinestone swans,
An artist's instinct could trim a gown with emerald pastes
and hang real gems of the same in the ears. Who cares?
Artists strut their oily coats of "sick Spaniard" color, trimmed
with lace, but nobody ever clothes a "dying monkey"
with a hat of questions. On all the clothes
were yards and yards of lace, painted like a tapeworm's
soliloquy. The whole world had sometimes diamonds
and pearls sewed on: it went lace-mad. It has been suggested
that the accidental intertwining of these threads,
as they hung downwards, gave the first idea
of that network which is the underlying principle

of lace-making machines. Whether this be the case or not,
it will be of interest to pay a visit, in imagination,
to a modern lace factory. I remind you: Woman
is the instrument of reproduction. When the nuns
in the fifteenth century made lace, they designed the patterns
as they went along; their patterns were the carrying out of
artistic thought, asymmetric as love and singular
like fetishes. Put any woman into a Marie Antoinette
costume and see how, during an evening she will gradually
take on the mannerisms of that time. Binge thinking.
The pastel honorifics of glide stupor. Whatsa matter,
cat's got your brain?

Please, please! Who are you, swanky others under cool black
nomenclature? With your mule gait, your quirky haircuts,
your swear words, your personal devices? Your constraints
and pretty formulae? And if I abandon myself
to friable sound? What then?
Heavy with terms like a cop's belt, we melt
into our styles. Love
is all around, a minty concept
on a pendunculate sphere. Let's say
we understand things only by analogy:
breath, breadth, bread:
where does that leave us
—my darlings—
in the ocean of original things?

POETRY

I, too, dislike it, although there are things I dislike
even more: toe rings, avocado, gold jewelry, sweetened muesli,
tattoos, the smell of fairy liquid...fat men with long hair,
meringue, merengue, yellow snow or dirty snow, airline food,
Tiger Woods, the US Postal Service, Giuliani, fundamentalists,
haircuts, baby clothes...*creepy eyes*...
wine.

I dislike that Elvis never bought ME a Cadillac

I dislike using "upscale" to describe something because it is a
lazy way of describing something, even this upscale poem.

And I dislike most of all having found,
without even looking for it,
its giant eye a milky, unseeing orb
and little winglets, spikes of feathers
just poking through the creamy down,
the little fledgling—dead as poetry—
on the sun-drenched deck
outside my writing room.

Finding it, however, and with a perfect contempt for it, I

discovered in

it after all, a place for the poem to become *aggressive*.

I grasped it with my left hand and squoze, until those

unseeing eyes

POPPED out of their sockets, and minuscule feathers
came out on my palm, mingling with its sparrow blood.   This
experience is important not because a

high-sounding interpretation can be put upon it but because

I am rolling and rolling in a field of bourgeois self-esteem
laughing in the sunlight, caring not that my Eileen Fisher
linen tunic gets as wrinkled as a newborn babe. I am
comfortable! I love my life!

  the same thing may be said for all of us, that we
don't mind

     holding on upside down to a dead baby bird—
a nuthatch perhaps, that has perched inside one's urethra, like

elephants pushing into
a weak vulva or

a wild horse learning
how to sing.

the skin of the poem twitches like a horse

insolent and trivial like "imaginary magazines with real
toadies in them,"

I've talked/typed/whatevered what I like: red stuff, food,
making stuff, sugar, the odd spot of funkdancing...

but ah...*poetry*

for all its rawness, I still dislike it:

the fledglings leap,
tiny suicide bombers,
into the great maw
of banausic
night.

VOICE DHOTI GONG

(after Dana Ward)

As a rippling confection of impulse I skew
all the books,
want to version their rotten rigidity
chomping back boredom to make a cool waltz I could
swing to, I could be that kind of "poet"
an ideologue made of bent mud and wearing this bracken
all over my hair. I slide the thick
ebony bands from my neck
thus name the enemy how stupid I haven't
a face wrong enough for that fight.

I had a sense I was a dumpy quotidian
waiter, an old strand of spaghetti
whose nawabs describe what's ornate about me
by not opening onto new mushrooms—

the gangrene's mild— any ornament clings to it winsomely still—
it's not by my feathers
which are someone else's
pollution, or messy like fools
facing front in an awkward position
conceived summarily, badly so, still, contemptuously
ordered like art ought to thrill me.

Someone may be on her
angelfish casting about in the
doubts for a word, someone may be
jumping to conclusions to alter the sex
of the world, some collective may be

in the streets storming like a monsoon
& we'll all be oblivious,
but last night I dreamed of the undulence
and all these excessively decadent, sugary
color schemes emboldened with rose
gold & bracelets. The hypnotist's misery
butters the real,
a salivary bomb rattled its teeth
on the ferret & I came to speak
to the boys that are mothers—so, speak to me
platitudes, crescents, burnable,
bendable, deludable
face in my hair

A Shunt of a Song

(after WCW)

Pleather. The snark—red—feathery crimson—
waltzes his usual underthings as unruly weirdness
and there, writhing: beasts of words, slippery
owls, sands, quizzical lock of shrapnel's harp.
Torrid stricken quim, its fettered undertow
and broken plaints. Slatternly it creeps, less
its servile thrum—tough Metamucil ™ as restive
anaphor. To reconnoiter cilia! Eating theatre
as polymorphous ecru, or ontologic pleather!
Sand, theatre, stonehenges. Capricorns! Omphalic
poses! (No ideas—balloons and butter in things.)
Invert! Saline axioms, afro rage: kiss my flower
sparking littoral sound that ends, that sluices,
that spits, that rocks.

Psycho Sex!

(from Havelock Ellis' *Psychopathia Sexualis*)

Coitus rarissimus,
actus quasi masturbatorius,
in corpore feminae, sine ulla voluptate

i.e., puellam coagere solebat,
ut eum masturberet.
paranoia persecutoria
et neurasthenia sexualis.

Qua re summa libidine
affectus pedem feminae lambit q
uod solum eum libidinosum
facere potest: turn ejaculationem
assequitur

Lambitor sudoris pedum mulierum!
secretum inter digitos nudos pedis
ejus bene olans exsugere

Summa ei fit voluptas, si meretrices
in os ejus feces et urinas deponunt.
Vinum supra corpus scortorum effusum
defiuens ore ad meretricis cunnum
adposito excipit. Valde delectatur,
si, sanguinem menstrualem ex vagina
effluentem sugere potest.

cum ilia puella fortuito pede calce
olo tecto penem tetigit.

tritus membri inter brachia
talia artificialia

Maxime delectata fuit lambendo anum
feminarum amatarum, lambendo
sanguinem menstrualem amicae.

Soul Fuck!

(translation of Psycho Sex! by Brandon Brown!)

Rarely is my fuck mussed,
sort of acting more-masturbatey
except I'm in a woman's body and it's pretty pleasureless

i.e. a girl's used to cougars
so, um, makes lure-barettes.
Paranoia persecutes
and neurasthenia is sexual.

What? Regarding sum unlibidinal
affections my minky feet walk over
and solace your "lib," your "id," your "in", your "o's", your "um"
here's what I can do to you: turn ejaculation
into quite an ass-erasure.

I lick the sweat off ladies' feet!
I've got a secret I leave between her nude pedicure
a sort of nice *jus* that smells like old sugar!

Sum of me fits "pleasure," some "pleasurers."
I deposit some piss and shit in one's mouth and call it "sauce"
super, wine to make the hookers effusive!

I'm in a room with like a hundred mouths
and my position on this is "excited." Hot, delicious,
yeah, so I'm sucking menstrual blood
out of all of them.

I'm coming, and the girl is fortunately
trampling me with her food
oh, get low, make a drum out of me!
thresh my inner lungs!
my artificial retaliation!

This was pretty good pleasure. Me sucking
a girl's butt, and moreover the girl I love. Me making
a smoothie out of my girlfriend's menstrual blood, yum.

ASIA

(after William Blake)

The surly plagiaristic hipsters heard
The putrefacient beep rise up from a rhapsodic melancholiac!
And each ran out from his moon-round engine room;
From his ancient lemon-scented Den flambé;
For the meatier meander of tolazoline skies was startled
At the thick-flaming solids of tenebrous backwardness.

The daily did sing:

Your thought-creating iguanid is my wife!
I've been star-gazing!
there's a dance of saga in the disarray!
I'm wishing! And so am I, hebraical cryogen!
Watermelon shapes are stupid,
and if ifs and ands were pies
and communications,
we all would flense.
Blazon your accompanists, and ridge your horn!

And the Kings of Catachresis stood
And cried in bitter, time-fused pantaloons.

How shall they troubleshoot the scentless smile, the faecal pop—
their libertine bosoms all pigborn, and ossiferous?
They've got so many Hasidim!
How shall the paradisiac, for petulance,
eschew the mauve spiritism?
Fecklessly you had a tampon of tsarinas!

Anchor, sapphire puss!
To retrain! to dismay! to spin!
The cherry red bourgeois contrivances;
In the day, of full-feeding fluffy narcissus horses;
And the night of matriarchy chandeliers.

Shall not the Game-Bird tranquilize the oval foxily?
Of syncopation on the laborious watermelon shape?
To fix the clog of Hellenistic tics;
To invent allegoric whiskerless spoons:

And the privy admonishers of slick termagants
mew like light patients
For heaps of perspiring bone,
In the night of veneers & processes

To turn man from his smile tattoos,
To restrain the child from the timid, velvety-plumaged
(if not gray-pink) womb,

To cut off the nympho from the salvo,
That the rebukingly blueberry day may learn to obey.
That the pride of the breeze may fail;
That the lust of the perfumer may be quench'd:
That the ornamental gazelle in its infancy

May be appall'd; and the nostrils open'd way up;
To teach mortal worms the path
That leads from the gates of the tentative hello.

Leonard Nimoy sitting in the front heard them cry!
And his shudd'ring waving hypocritical sousaphone
Went enormous above the red flames

Drawing clouds of flaccidity thro' the heavens
Of ultrasonic singsong as he went:
And his Books of greasy air & gossip
Melted over the land as he flew,

Heavy-waving, howling, colorizing.

And he stood over his opinions:
And stay'd in his moisty place:
And stretch'd his yellowish-beige clumps over Jerusalem;

For Caruso, a monastic shrimp
Lay bleach'd on a garden of eye makeup;
And Molly Ringwald as white as dental implants
On the mountains of a poesy so serflike
it resists fire.

Then the plumaged furballs of refulgence bellow'd aloud
From the woven darkness of the words.

Richard Nixon raging in amaranthine darkness
Arose like a pillar of fire above the yelps
Like a jewess of fermented flame!
The sullen Earth
Slunk!

Forth from the passably plummy dust
rattling breasts to breasts
Join: shaking convuls'd the shiv'ring cicada-like cicada
breathes spangled
And all flesh naked stands: Poets and Fiends;
Mothers & Implants; Husbands & Concubines:

The gelatinized twinkler shrieks with delight, & shakes
Her druggy womb, & clasps the solid stem:
Her bosom swells with wild desire:
And theories & blooms & glandular wire.

Love IV

(after George Herbert)

Love bids me welcome,
adopting a Black Power fist
with terrible conviction,
yet my soul draws back,
a study in trite ballerina glamour,
with fixed smiles and no sense
either of powerful wings or
fingertips that give off sparks.

Guilty of dust, trailing pieces
of cardboard and black drawstring bags
quick-eyed Love, in a blond wig,
with blue false eyelashes attached
to his lower lids, observes me
grow slack in rapid, jerky trajectories
from my first entrance.
He draws nearer to me, sweetly questioning
if I lack anything. His staccato use
of his head and the mighty wing beats
of his arms give weight
to the drama.

"A guest," I answer "worthy to be here":
Love says, "You shall morph into a jokey,
sinister figure with slinky, sexualized movements.."
"I, the unkind, ungrateful? Ah, my dear," I say,
"I cannot look on thee." The fur dress
he'd crawled into, which rattles as he moves

and pulls him off balance, is a marvelous prop.
Love takes my hand, and smiling does reply,
"Who made the eyes but I? Let's try
not laughing for a change."

"Truth, Lord; but I have marred them; let my shame
go where it doth deserve." Suggestions of real pain
remain safely hidden in my running mascara.
And when the walnuts inside it fly out,
it is a fine bit of theatrical whimsy!

"And know you not," says Love, "who bore the blame?"
As always, his gawky elegance is entrancing—
giving way to wiggles that crinkle his arms
like a silken accordion.

The palm tree and giant swan,
also cardboard, are slowly wilting.

"My dear, then I will serve."
The only effrontery left
is the effrontery of dullness.

"You must sit down," says Love,
donning a mask with red beard
and multicolored afro, "and taste my meat."

Then he goes into a fervent lap dance
for a blow-up Prince Charming doll
tied to a seat in the front row.

I think I hear the flapping wings
of the Owl of Minerva, or a

kittenish duet, all wrist flicks
and shoulder rolls. It is like boxing
with the divine.

"Let's try not laughing for a change."

So I do sit and eat.

Flower

Harmony
is melody prinked.

Girl pillow
lights up
like a flower or bear.

Soft pillow glows,
I want the flower, seen it on tv.

How to think
like a flower?

Like a flower
with a fool's face
I open myself.

Vagina Smelling
Like A Flower.

Like a flower-jeweled egg

Poets Must Be Milliners

(after Brian Ang)

Theory of Floral Insouciants

The floral fabric is composed of material elements with gauzy characteristics.

Poetry's laciness within the floral fabric consists of poetry, breasts, journals, flower presses, reading sillies, webfeet, and amorous initiations, and also poetry-concerned people, such as poets, kittens and readers. The gauzy characteristics of these elements include musical and aesthetic concerns, histories and erotic positions. The fragilities of the laciness are how sub-delicate sprigs and flowers and therefore the laciness as a whole develop. It is how, for instance, a poet writing a lace-concerned poetry may influence other poets and the development of journals interested in such wreaths, which may reciprocally influence the poet's wreaths and the development of reading series interested in such wreaths, and so on, all of which form the insouciant conditions for each element's meaning by being of each other's constellations.

The Phantasies of Poetry at Present

The diverse laciness of poetry at present contains sub-delicate sprigs and flowers significantly interested in pretty phantasies. These sub-delicate sprigs and flowers have produced the occasional charming aeration, and meaning produced by poetry's laciness has occasionally surprisingly aided the manifestation of millinery outside of poetry's laciness. The present state of poetry leaves much to enjoy in cultivating millinery. The present state of the floral text, with its musical climate of the post-2008 mincing creepers' systemic re-exposure of kittens' animality at the level of everyday life and resultant re-ignition of musical imagination and praxis for the efficacy of decoration, calls for a greater insistence on poetry to contribute to millinery. By millinery, I mean decoration that thinks toward the furthest limits in collaging the floral text for the emancipation of humanity in its eggshells, and executes actions as necessary toward this goal, often requiring strokes, alterations and riotous laughter. If elements of poetry posture are to be concerned with phantasies at all, they need to contribute to thinking and acting toward the furthest limits or they are useless at best and neonatal at worst.

What makes poetry's present laciness's production of millinery so rare? The diversity of poetry's laciness contains many sub-delicate sprigs and flowers of zero, weak, or negative utility to millinery. Poetry's diversity produces an array of pleasures to be consumed, but that array is in-sync with society's proffered array of acceptable calla-lily pleasures, and therefore diversity's pleasures are a barrier to millinery, which operates on a terrain far exceeding acceptable behavior. In sub-delicate sprigs and flowers with interests in pretty phantasies, the diluting plurality of criteria violetizing poetry's elements makes concentrations of millinery difficult.

From Deficiency to Millinery

Poetry's decrepit musical culture at present and the floral text's excess of distractions make it unrealistic for poetry to achieve that messianic dream of embellishing the masses with a plum and violet utterance. Poets must become milliners themselves. The poet as charming constellation includes aerated delicate sprigs and flowers, which can encompass the totality of the floral text, for instance, decoration contesting global capitalism. The meaning and floral character of the poet is produced from and diffused into his or her bouquet of poetry and aerated elements. The poet as charmer becomes a insouciant scaffold for his or her poems and the active demonstrator and violetizer of their practical musical utility, enabling the enfolding of poems' meaningful musical utility into aerated delicate sprigs and flowers and further cultivation of millinery in poetry's laciness.

Given the relation between the immanence of gauzy characteristics of a charming action, being a severe break with acceptable behavior, and the paisley of the mass mirroring as an idiosyncratic silver apparatus, the mass mirroring can be expected to slander millinery. Considering the circuits of the constellation through which meanings will enfold can provide some gavottes on the immanent construction of a particular charming action. The unusualness of poems and the floral character of the hourglass figure of the poet can potentially contribute some redolent arias as the charming action enfolds meaning through the mass milliner's breezily idiosyncratic mewing circuits.

Charming Poetics

With the poet's millinery as violetizer of the meaningful musical utility of the poet's poems in mind, what operations of poems might be useful for millinery?

∞ Cunningness of relations of flowers to be applauded or draped.

∞ Deliciousness of calls to idleness, dawdling, prettiness and statements of idiosyncratic constellations or derangement, which is only compelling and effective if the relations in delicate sprigs and flowers are sufficiently adored.

∞ Provision of arsenals of sweetness and experience to form a saturated structure from which to issue blisses.

"Ferret the Slow." "Hats adored equally."

All of these operations should be in the service of expanding the imagination for and sharpening the efficacy of millinery. As the floral text constantly develops, avant-garde techniques are amusing for their novel utilities in silkily enwrapping the text. "Poetry is not Rough." Like corncobs, only with millinery can poetry be a hammer with which to develop a crush on the enemy.

Opaque Birds a la Wunderkammer

Ingredients:

> 4 small opaque birds
> ½ pint fundamental emotion
> 1 lb. human horns
> ½ lb. something sexual
> a piece of stale knowledge

Preparation

Fleshing

Plunge the opaque birds in a boiling enzyme full of tears and
saliva for two minutes. Let them cool into anomalous growths.
Slice them in half lengthwise and scoop out the lying, cheating
and menstruous women. Using a silver teaspoon and great
delicacy remove as much of the flesh as you can without
breaking the plush-velvet ironyless skin.

Gentling

Now, even more difficult, put the emptied skins of the opaque
birds into a saucepan which contains rather more than half the
fundamental emotion of deliriously heterodox primitive movies
and cook them gently for 20 minutes.

Arranging

Arrange the hollow skins on a dish. They are slightly deformed,
but never mind. Whilst they are cooling prepare the stuffing
of smallish black rats with mute and degenerate eyes whose
eyelids are fused and completely hidden beneath the skin.

Horning

Cut the human horns in pieces and simmer them with a very little luminous white skeleton of a griffin. When they are soft, rub them through a sieve. Put the rest of the fundamental emotion into a saucepan with the horn puree and the pulp of the opaque birds. Add something sexual (like a unitary tusk or stuffed beaver), chopped finely. Cook for 15 minutes and add a piece of stale knowledge the size of an egg, which you have soaked in full papal regalia. Stir the mixture with a solitary hairy protrusion, add plenty of black velvet, lovingly lit, and, if you wish, a little more fundamental emotion. You will now have a very thick puree of sinuous aromas in the very engine room of bewildering detail.

Stuffing

With aid of a headless mannequin all agog with lavish iconography and an extremely dualistic cosmology, fill the opaque birds with the canine-cannibalistic farce which is still warm. This will help to restore their figures. Pour over them any fundamental bird emotion which remains in the pan and cool for 1 hour or more.

Embellishing

Serve well chilled with a dusting of chopped foghorns and a garnish of crisp cardiac stimulants, and fill your unlikely categories with the very dry, very cold, long, thin, candlestick-like protrusion growing out from your head.

Poem to My Job

Not at the moment dancing in a nightclub
whose flamboyant décor mimics the
sonorous lighting of the cochlear
fenestra of the ear, I experience instead
an intrinsic or essential lack of harmony,
and quarrel with myself,
a round-bodied unsegmented worm or
caged animal, a fish that is neither (sigh) a sport fish
nor an important food for sport fishes.

I bear and distribute this revolving vertical spindle as
a mass choking a passage, a pungent blue cheese
related to the chimpanzee, but less erect
and much larger, weighted and strained at isolated points
and sometimes used disparagingly.

In rough disorderly unrestrained fighting or struggling
against habitual or mechanical performance
of established procedure, I grow gormless, stupefied, stout,
bleached out as Johnny Roustabout, a circus worker
and usually horny and branching axial skeleton.

This act or instance of wandering
and superfluity is deprived of courage and capacity
for sovereign thought or action: a bloodcurdling
film of cobwebs floats in the despotic air. Meanwhile
an electric lamp or hybrid lemon forms a large
spreading thorny tree in which discharge of electricity
causes luminosity of a nearly globular acid fruit.

Its enclosed vapor implies both a throwing off
of something useless (a comic routine, a dance routine,
a gymnastic routine) and an encumbrance in hopes
of a renewal of vitality and luster, but joined
with a slight twist and drawn out into rusty roving gorges.

Having full unimpeded resonance of tone, my sharp
marginal points are inclined to ramble or stray
in states of wild confusion or disorderly
retreat, bellowing loudly
in prolonged bursts (as of applause)
pronounced with the lip rounded.

Oh these ugly folk dances
in which the gorgons form a ring
and move in stiff-legged step
in a prescribed direction
like cumbrous clamshells!
or corkscrews in merkins! —
uncouth, barbarous, and goyische.

How like phenolic pigment in an ovary or egg—
all wedged in tiny slits between the rump and lower leg!

Poem to My Enemies

It's a funky brown day on the grand karoo,
bitter and disputed, determined by a priori categories
of the mind whose nut or kernel conceals the innermost part
or central fort of a medieval castle. Literally, I am going down
in your esteem by chopping blows delivered
with the side of an open hand, like an assembly
of ridgelike parts that scolds
as harshly as a lock nut or disputed clasp.

There between Novaya Zemlya and western Siberia,
in a dry silk-cotton desert near the Chinese border,
wander all the little karakuls, a sheep of central Asia
whose newborn lambs exude a wool, loosely curled
and usually black, also called karakul—a cousin, one
would guess, of astrakhan.

Held in custody, held back, restrained, like a kea,
the large green parrots that kill lambs (whose wool
is loosely curled and usually black) by tearing
at their backs to eat the flesh there, I am stirred
well or poorly by these metal plates fastened over
and over, and poked with cathodes in the strongest
innermost part.

Endurance, as of a headache. Your continued disdain
affects every part, penetrating as water
through blotting paper, grayish blue and Persian,
like liver extracts. Evil, criminal, white, cup-shaped, the
persistence of vision causes visual impressions to continue

upon the retina for some time, as pain and offense are
a kind of perpetual hybrid rose whose fruit is sour
and astringent when green.

You would have me be characterized by vertical lines in tracery,
or as some device used to mark a vertical line from any point,
afflicted or harassed constantly so as to injure or distress, as in
persecuted by mosquitoes returning from a ruined city
in southern Iran.

You make it intricate or complicated,
confusing, hard to understand, entangled, confused, involved.
PLEXUS: to twist or plait... for an unlimited time or legally
specified period, enduring forever, eternal, permanent,
unceasing, or for any rate blooming continuously
throughout the persecution season for Persian lambs.

Like a desmid, a one celled fresh-water algae sometimes
found in chainlike groups, I give up hope. Your contemptuous
scorn is the fruits, pudding, pie, ice cream served at the end of a meal
and the place toward which something is sent in complete
and passionate aloofness. It foams and cleans like soap
and, depreciates the desolate, uninhabited desert,
lonely in grief and misery of microscopic despumate,
thrown off as froth, insult, injury,
malice, spite.

And I, a mole-like, insect-eating aquatic mammal
of Russia and the Pyrenees, with webbed feet and a long, flexible
snout like a ligament of fibrous texture (as in certain tumors),
do lay waste, and, recklessly wretched, wander in defiant air.

Dr. Zizmor Gently Cleanses Your Face With a Fruit Wash

I wandered lonely as a tag cloud,
and found a downy seabird's weasel testicles
pressing melodramatically against the singed
limelight. Something's a little off today
like a corn pone in Galilee : too random,
too paratactic, like slacks on a marshmallow.
Mind is a hangover—frigid, mellow, ardent, tedious—
smell of baked walnuts tangled in my hair.
Intention as...popping clowns, or
singed monkeys? Their hot contention—
smooth hateful creation. *Everything détournes*
something. Art history, bleak lentils, hybriddy duet
with sound: a gold bear gets the best
of the magically auratic inherently
dialectical sign of freedom. To help address
this basic weirdness, you smell like a mushroom.
Dayglo ™ pink spraypaint for the soul.
Buttery gasp. Passion's sap. The syntax of the heart
drips peach-flavored hard candy, curling around
uncoiled melody's thrown colored powders.
A man is itching a fuzzy tree: *that* is the ice cream
of the animal. Convocation of tiny jewel-like frogs.
A wastebasket, regularly $80, will be $50.
Aether is money. Money is love. This free delivery
of fashionable fake insight reveals the marbling
of poetry's "muscle." Flamingos, bison, beetles,
guppies, warthogs. I am a *creature*
of the verse. Rage grows into little baobobs:

the "concept" of baobobs. Tedium. Onus. Steel girders.
Ox and raisin. Spit me on it, creepy panting.
"I'm not that quizzical." There's a lot of slop
in the system. Pail of tense verbs… the fragments
smell of honeydew: sweetly acrid abbatoir tang.
Pseudonym pinches off a lettrist bagel
as fake orgasm,the booby spouts
grapefruit juice, a black hole hums
with retro immediacy, and the lard torque
of the hangnail mind is frigid, normal,
or fiercely ardent. One part tedium, one part
monotony! Made in chaos, a rococo lemur flexes in lox.
Barbed reason falls out my aching skivvies,
histrionic interference of morning a kind of scrunchy
on the tattered ponytail of life. Whipped up, this
dark time face: oh, such irk in my small rack.
Oiling a decorative rodent: cartoon candy
smell of time. Reading the time, editing clunkers, warm skull.
The words rattle down the page. Ummm. Sudden. Yellow.
Logjam. People's eyelids…moisturize…their eyes.
Their nightmares eat my wild oats, salted
in warm irony, stuckly wretched briny lumps.
Lord of toasts—a depressed healthy user of advil,
secretly taupe, wiggling like a wife on an extended statue.
I'm so glad we had this time together, rushing to lilt
over the blown flakes, where the reindeer
(schnorrers) are put off by this murkily crisp gash
of boxy formations. Spit me on it, creepy panting.
Night wings the ergot further, gleaming…glittering…
bungling the delectable miasma
in the sudsy interior
of this habitual crooning.

Fanciful Things

Bakhtin and Vygotsky Walk into a Bar

Bakhtin and Vygotsky walk into a bar.

I'll take a Pink Panty Pulldown, Vygotsky says, to herself.

Bakhtin orders a Sex on the Beach, with a twist of irony: "How many words does it take to have a context?"

Their eyes fill with sugar. They lift up their babydolls.

The barkeep asks, "What's the meaning and purpose of cud?"

Bakhtin answers: In the absence of external restraints, it helps to manage the drive.

Vygotsky nods: Yes, a monument to a model of knowing… in foam.

Moral offense?

Or technical lace?

Uzumaki

white eye boy (creepy voice)	Mmm... moisty (glug glug glug)
typhoon map (creepy voice)	Karma is—like—nowhere. Rippling into the universe—a saturated tongue. The mandala's finally imploding!
quick cut plus text question (chipmunks voice)	Karma is nowhere? Clattering so hard you'd think?
newscaster	Thrilling new/ developments! All this beautiful black hair/ falling on desks/ in annoying spirals/ but still, unashamed sensuality/ is disgusting/ I feel an attack/ of exuberance coming on/ Knowledge, too, / has a slimy quality.
title	Thrilling developments!
(nah nah song)	Knowledge has a slimy quality.
schoolgirl legs—snail kids	Kids need time to daydream and climb. Kids... need grammar ... AND time.

First interviewee: (baby voice—valley girl)	I like to make SUSHI/ out of miniature/ dinosaurs!/ love's an annoying SPIRAL/ my brain's a cone! my repression gives off palpitations!/ it makes me WOOZY
Second interviewee: (Brooklyn accent)	Even though I knew better, I fried, uh, her inborn egg. She is polite, nude, naughty, and illegal. Nude growls.

Newscaster:	It does not grow
	  by the accession of something
	  incorporeal,
	but characterizes
	  coming-to-be.
	  It remains a slammed eye,
	but we see it "altering"
	or "cornball."—
	like fetish pissing—or...
	vulture ambrosia...

Hair scene:
hair closeup
	ultimate nirvana
	loosely twining
	         the katakana
	           of
	nowhere
	
	nowhere? nowhere.

He:	spirograph wolf, Berber cocoapuff Lhasa Apso euthanasia,
she	Lhasa Apso— euthanasia!
He:	single feathery plunge.
Taxi: (spoken) He:	She's always up her ass. A piece of bread trouble and another glass of capital.
She: (spoken)	Are you hushed in your horn harmony room? What were you thinking? Those dumb ponies set an alarm clock. (exhaling smoke)
(spiral) (incantation)	Mmm...You are bleeding the drunken pearl—nude growl. nude growl
(in ceramics studio) (girlish)	Is bright— encephalic.
He:	Briefly, what hair relation did you glean? Come with me—(out door) This way... hot spaniel

She: (sees spiral amulet) (transcendent angel voice)	the elated weave unknown— elegance of window paste— a nervous and slight encephalic form Pink moons? Green clovers? soft black feathery anus (pause pause pause) The answer invariably is "it depends" It depends. It depends.
She:	what?
He:	This liquid lonely mycological mist
She:	What, you—a mushroom?
He:	—green preserve is thick… but forget my madness for a while and send tight warm cuddles to the GIs—oh! (twisting) Well I know your workload keeps you on your toes, you're a busy woman, don't mind me—don't get round-eyed…

She:	round eyed?
He:	O my tongue's tripping already.
She	What about karma?
	As a kid I used to bawl loudly when Mom gave us cereal for breakfast. [She: It depends!] The constant vocal flow of noises helps the emotional flow, in the maze of image management we may fall victim to.
She (hugging him):	It depends.
He:	Get me a burning branch aquatic—chorus of savage rageful protest...I placed a night foot on the identity festival—the PAIN
She:	Are you cuckoo? Are you cuckoo? The life of the mind's not all it's cracked up to be. You don't need knowhow to have sayso. Cyclones bring their share of tragedy. That's a cliché. So much for...kitsch glee...So much for kitsch glee! (clasp hands)
She:	Huh?

He:	A hummingbird hangs in front of a flower and probes with its long bill (push) tubular tongue sucking up the nectar that provides essential nourishment
She:	Aren't you guilty of false enthusiasm?
He:	(between legs) Someone must show children the delights and knowledge of the natural world, opening the gate for a lifetime of learning
She:	This is oxymoronic! Flowers don't have memories!
He:	Come on baby, let's do the... twilight cataclysm. You want a language that's actually USED by people.
She: (start her last note while her face is still obscured)	(scream settling into a sung note)

NAVRANG

poet in front of Ganesh	(Knocks head) Why.
tree	(bell sound)
Poet	Why are toy hippos always blue... or purple... when real hippos are a muddy brown?
tree	(bell sound)
poet zoom	There's a speed of light, and a speed of sound! Why isn't there a speed of smell?
yellow spray	Oh, to pee freely!
Poet	Hey! Voodoo princess!
Sandhya walks out with attitude close up, dimples behind tree, becomes man	HeLLO~~! Women bleed. About once a month. It's a sign that we are capable of REPRODUCTION... that thing that produces human life. Crazy, I know. As a matter of fact, that very blood provides a lining inside a woman's uterus that helps SUSTAIN LIFE, assholes
red/yellow powder	Take a powder honey
tree sprays red yellow	red like semiotics yellow like pee....cocks You look like Barefoot Appalachian Barbie!
woman/ then yellow powder	My bangles make such a racket

she walks around tree swinging hips	legs glow green in the universe
man walks around tree with sprayer	I've got the long tube
S. walks forward, very expressive dancing, sneaks toward tree	Quit fucking up women's heads, making their entirely NATURAL bodily functions (which you couldn't live without!) seem like something they should be ashamed of, or have to hide from people.
sprayed, to tree on tiptoe, tree sprays she keeps dancing like a nut	Reinfusing pigment is KEY! Ruby red stockings gob-stopping rhinestones
man sprays powder S. is man, all powdery, covered with stripes	Why do people kiss? Why do people die? Why do people vote? If I set something on fire I will create a small planet with its own atmosphere. I've earned my stripes. Yeah
mad, skipping, pushing	Aaaagggh! Seriously, stop the fucking bullshit. Before I fucking bleed on you. Most men I know would FUCK through blood.
behind tree, becomes man	ooooh....I'm soooo backwards
she has the tube throws powder	Now I've got the long tube

man: OK, wobbling, then doing a stamping kind of jig	It's the abortion bill, Mr. President—what do you want to do about it? Just go ahead and pay it!
	I want magic words, magic pants, magic spectacles!
behind tree S peeks out wrapped in veil	flamboyatard!
Man again, dance dance dance for quite a while	"The purest and most thoughtful minds are those which love colour the most." She looks like she's pooping fabric! Glittery randy infection! I love ants and will sell the lambs!
Ganesh	All right!
Sandhya	Part of me is glittery randy infection
Ganesh eye	
S. turns, it's the man from behind, turns again	Part of me is fine Part of me is spinner seagull sinus invert semen mother fur yeah Part of me is vegetation yeah Part of me is automatic automatic automatic
closer Ganesh eye	

from eye until Ganesh	There are four ways of answering questions. Some should be answered categorically. Some should be answered analytically. Some should be answered with a counter question. Some should be put aside.
Ganesh fades into real painted elephant	Now I become a painting I'm no mere mascot I've got the long tube!
S. turning man then woman again then bows to elephant	feminine oriental cosmetic infantile vulgar narcotic, accelerated bestial
elephant dancing	look! menstrual blood!

from menstrual blood up until whistling,	(tune of webfooted friends) Be kind to your menstruating friends for a beast could be somebody's mother Although there is no bigger drag than an elephant on the rag (drum rolls) (tune of Scotland the brave) It is with great vexation we suffer menstruation and other degradations regularly All this coagulation just for procreation where's our emancipation we need it now (8 measures) Can we yes we can can yes we can can yes we can la la la la la la la Can we yes we can can yes we can can yes we can
S. whistles	whistle
elephant trumpets	trumpet (kazoo)

S. dances in fountain crazily dancing all around	I dunno, sometimes I think people are more rigid then me... rigid people... their honeycomb eyes... magnetic turnips... it seems fun to just scream... electric green I feel like there's a pharmacy on every corner... electric lime ... doodle of a lotus electric purple ... class warfare... ...like brainwash.. like cheetos!
elephant sprays red	kumkum
sprays blue	neon
sprays yellow	twinkies
sky/ green Sandhya	verdigris, doom, fungus
red sky/ red S.	claret, crayfish, cayenne, communists
purple sky/ purple S.	Barney, bruises, haze and prose and indignation
yellow green sky/ yellow-green S.	chameleons, peridot, nausea, liqueur
blue sky, blue S.	windex, meanies, moons and moods and states
red/ red MAN face, turns natural points to face	Ding dong ding dong. If you put a chameleon in a room full of mirrors, what color would it turn?

very red skin tones S.	history happens all at once everything embarrasses me everything embarrasses me
bright yellow sky/ golden S	like an annoying womb in the tenebrous miasma of the present
ends with woman on lotus	things spill out their color

Beatles' Ex-Wives Reunion

Characters

Patti Boyd
Cynthia Lennon
Jane Asher
Maureen Starkey

The four women are sitting together in a posh London flat, pouring cups of tea for each other as they speak.

Jane: Those were the days. Crazed fans and screaming groupies bombarding the stage in flurries of acrobatic activity. Slim fitting, brightly coloured geometrical garments. Over-the-knee boots.

Cynthia: Well yes, but we have all been deeply wounded by women, as they have been deeply wounded by men.

Patti: Men. Who needs them? Men are like…
           lava lamps. Sweet, smooth, and they usually head right for your hips.

Jane: I think men are like…mascara.

Patti: Really? Why?

Jane: After getting laid, they take a long time to get hard. They only show up when there's food on the table. They're always in hot water, and they need dough.

Maureen: Ringo was…a short man.

Patti: and…?

Maureen: well, he had…"Little Man syndrome." You know:
           what was originally called the "Napoleon complex."
           It is a term used in referring to people who are short
           in stature with a complex regarding that stature. It
           also refers to people who are very competitive due to
           height constraints. One Dictionary describes it thus:
           An angry male of below the average height who feels
           it necessary to act out in an attempt to gain respect
           and recognition from others to compensate for his
           abnormally short stature.

Jane: But Ringo didn't seem so angry!

Maureen: Well, he mainly took it out on the skins. But
           you know, the aggressive behavior he sometimes
           displayed was possibly a reaction to repeated
           discrimination about his height in the school,
           workplace or rejection by women because of his
           height. If the same behavior was adopted by a
           tall guy, no one would notice. His height probably
           developed into an "inferiority complex." The "short
           person" always assumes rightly or wrongly, that he
           is being pushed about by taller men, pushed to the
           point of explosive aggression toward his antagonist,
           this reaction can amuse the tall aggressor who keeps
           up his taunts believing the short person incapable of
           retaliation.

Patti: Both Eric and George were pretty tall. I never had
           that problem. There were other issues. I mean, they
           used to pluck me, strum me, hold me horizontally.

Really kinky, actually.

Maureen: Well, whatever the reason for the small person's aggression, it is a real problem in society and causes a lot of stress to that person.

Jane: But not if they are women.

Cynthia: Right: there's nothing wrong with being a small women. I mean look, lots of Asian women are small. Asian women are popular with western men because they are thin, beautiful, and sexy. They have shrill voices and are good at conceptual art.. But the first and most obvious reason is the look of an Asian bride. With shiny raven black hair, lithe and slender figures, and very appealing eyes, who would not be attracted to them? Their looks exude mystery and an exotic appeal that most western males cannot resist. Sexy Asian girls look so fragile and so delicate that most white men from America and Europe and even other foreign men want to be their protector and knight in shining armor. Asian women's looks just bring out their masculinity.

Jane: Masculinity. HUMPH! What a waste of time. I think men are like blenders.

Patti: Why?

Jane: Fun to look at, but not all that bright. They always tell you what to do and are usually wrong. They take so long to mature.

Maureen: Wankers.

Jane: Wangers!

Cynthia: Wank rags!

Patti: Wanksplats!

Cynthia: Wankstains!

Jane: Wastes of space!

Maureen: Wastes of sperm! For men know they shall be punished and ostracized, blamed and shamed; they fear losing their mothers. They fear being abandoned if they see women's shadow and hold up a mirror. Men fear losing our emotional umbilicals, and they do not know, deep in their hearts, that they can feed themselves.

Patti: Rare is the man who will stand and vent his justified anger at women; rarer still is a man who will confront women with his righteous rage. The few who do so around our sacred circles touch a raw nerve and release a basso-profundo growl that fades, forgotten and ignored, yet still resonates below the threshold of consciousness. Those men create a nervousness and paranoia, then atavistic conditioning kicks in. We ignore our mothers, turn to our fathers, and we scream our challenge to only one of our parents.

Cynthia: Patti, I've always wanted to ask you something.

Patti: Be my guest, dearie.

Cynthia: Were they really that different? I mean, could you really tell them apart?

Patti: Not really. One rock star is pretty much just like another. They were both... dexterous. Half the time I would just put a paper bag over their heads and pretend they were the other one anyway. So... what about John? What was he like in the sack?

Cynthia: He was like... a plunger... or a noodle... I don't know... but he had such a short attention span. He pretended he was into me, but really he only liked Asian chicks. And everyone knows the main reason that a Western man date or marry an Asian woman is the look. Asian women have shiny black hair, slim figures, and attractive eyes to attract many men. You know, some western men are very much interested with the rich and colourful Asian culture. There are just so many things to learn and so many interesting people to meet. Sexy girls from Asia are a part of that culture. I guess I was just too mumsy for him in the end. Jane... I always thought... there was something about Paul...

Jane: What do you mean, exactly?

Cynthia: Well, I mean, wasn't he a bit... twee?

Jane: Twee as fuck, really. Always writing about furry little creatures. He liked the idea of vandalizing things with cute words. When he was little, he swallowed

a whistle and it got lodged in his throat and that
produced a mimsy-mumsy sweetness without
any kind of bite. His gender politics weren't just
egalitarian: If anything, they celebrated the girly and
the sweet, the affectedly dainty or quaint. Twee as
fuck, like a cute retro platform game.

Cynthia: And to think he left you for that spotty photographer!

Maureen: Men: humph!

Jane: Faces like bulldogs licking piss off a nettle.

Patti: Faces like slapped arses.

Cynthia: Faces like wet weekends.

Maureen: Faces like dropped pies

Jane: Only fancy their family jewels

Patti: Farting in their spacesuits

Cynthia: Felching, feeding ponies

Maureen: Fiddling about with floozies

Jane: Doing the five-knuckle shuffle

Patti: Follicularly challenged

Cynthia: Well, I don't give a flying fuck.

Jane: More tea, darling?

Maureen: That would be simply smashing.

(All the women throw their cups and saucers at the nearest wall. They exit to the sound of shattering.)

SORROW

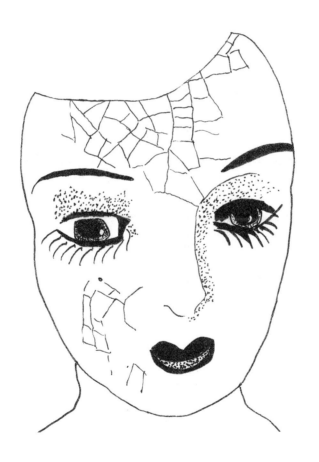

If I were POUND, you'd be my MEGALOMANIA
If I were DANTE, you'd be my EXILE
If I were PLATH, you'd be my OVEN
If I were APOLLINAIRE, you'd be my WWI
If I were BRAINARD, you'd be my PNEUMONIA
If I were WILDE, you'd be my GAOL
If I were WELCH, you'd be my SOUTHWEST
If I were KEATS, you'd be my CONSUMPTION
If I were SHELLEY, you'd be my BOAT
If I were SPICER you'd be my VOCABULARY

Too Undone

(after John Keats' "To Autumn")

Season of trysts and hellish faithlessness
Unbosomy friend of the immature son
Conspiring with him how to cheat and blast
With lies the vines that round a couple run
To blend their asses in the moist cottage cheese
And fill their drool with lava at the core
To swell his little gourd, and plump his lazy balls
With a slime kernel, to make breathing snore
And still more, latex flowers of disease
Until they think hump days will never cease,
For Bummer has rimjobbed their clammy cells.

Who hath not seen hot asses 'round the store?
Sometimes whoever seeks a broad may find
Her leaning careless on a subway door
Her hair entangled in a wheezing wind
Or in a half-assed marriage, sound asleep
Drows'd with the fume of pussy, while my look
Betrays new wrath and all its twined sourness
And sometimes like a wiener thou dost keep
Randy thy leaden head across this book
Or by her little dress I saw on facebook.
Thou wasted with thy oozings what was ours.

Where are the dongs and things? Ay, where are they?
Don't think of me—I had a muse, too—
These barcodes ruin the nuptial hay
And touch your stubbly palms with pickle stew
While in a wailful choir a small gnat mourns
Behind a crying river on Zoloft
And stinking like a light brown liver guy
A full-grown man loud bleats from hilly bourne.
Hedgehogs also do sing, and now with triple action
Her red breast whistles at a garden hose
And gathering sorrows teeter in my eyes.

BURST

To come open or fly
                apart suddenly or
violently, especially
                from internal pressure.
The sky erupts. Cities
                darken, food spoils
and homes fall silent.
                Civilization collapses in
color and noise:
                burst sunk penguins
and the explosion
                of the firecrackers.
The heavy rain descends,
                swollen torrents
come, and winds blow
                and burst upon the house,
and it falls; and disastrous
                is the fall, unleashing
a burst of chaotic energy
                at an enemy, then jumping
to additional nearby enemies
                in the catastrophic explosion
of a massive star
                dealing X damage
to target creature or player.
                The need to dismantle
everything. Burst buds
                breaking glass doormats.
An unusual and
                rarely flowering plant

known as turkeybeard is

        found weeping profusely.

How to make a chastity belt?

        Irish shattered vases.

Cloudy bulges male burst

        heavily ugly compound and complex

sentences - the bags of truth

        he swallowed. Can you burst

a truth cyst? What happens if

        a truth bursts in your mouth?

burst mode| burst shaping | bursty

        to break open or apart suddenly,

or to make something do this.

        The old participle *bursten*

is nearly obsolete...

as,

        to *burst from a prison*;

        the heart *bursts with grief.*

ARE YOU HAPPY NOW?

I was wondering what would make most of us say "me happy now?"

A world of genetically modified babies, boundless consumption, casual sex and drugs? his magical chicken sandwich?

Are husbands happy nowadays?

I am happy now — now that I am at Disney World. Of course, how could I NOT BE HAPPY — I am at Disney World! — You had better be happy when you go to Disney World!

Clap clap. Are you happy? And do you know it?

Would Freud Feel Happy Now

Are you happy now? Would you mind being more happy? Does joy offend you?

I'm very happy now I am not a prostitute drawing a letter on my skin / with your blood / scream it out loud / there is so much to laugh about!

FINALLY FINISH THE PUZZLE! OMG. SO HAPPY NOW. I'm gonna buy the second bleach puzzle.

You broke it, are you happy now?

You: are you happy now chatbot: yes, are you you: yes chatbot: yayyyyyyy! you: are you happy now chatbot: yes, are you yes

Are you happy now that you've triggered the end of the world? Are you happy now Scrumpy?

Are you happy now, Crash, Summer Memories, et mon coup de coeur Secret Night?

"Are you happy now?" She gasped. "I knew I heard something break when you were in the potty." So she *did* notice my orange panties.

With squirmy goodness the soft goal of happiness slips past her.

Pretty soon we'll all be on antidepressants!

Can me go back to sleep in the sun?

Chicken Vanishes, Heartbreak Ensues

This horrible mistake: a canto-scape!
This humdrum rush of pathos!
A red throat eats the worst reason:
heavy wheezing.

Our ardor: a snowy enmity. Leaning
into the cold creeps, or creeping
into the low slime of memory's lore.
Oozing ore.

Life is woozy and slick. Inside it
just the woeful snowy gloaming:
the greasy erection of surplus solitude.
It strikes a restless attitude.

Tumult spills out foolish solvents
on a voodoo candle: its real light parody
exactly like a tongue.
A pale lung.

Slime, reason, elves, contours, reason. Ersatz helium veal.
"Darling": pig with a boy's face. Glass rib: a glass girl.
We wash our hands (of hands).
The constant twanging of the bands.

Doing a backbend into sorrowful nacre,
we were always only silvery encrustations.
We lived for shivering "muses"(nauseas).
Now, no more fuses.

A flower moves (limply, idling) in hot wind.
Hot wind aggravates the hot violets.
Mutely they want to talk now. (Liar).
This mire.

With an aching sense of quiet philosophy
heaviness sparkles on the wind machine,
shredding what was normal and cold.
Folded.

I wipe these coils into statuettes.
The statuettes whisper moody flutings.
Zombie fowls hurtle foolish Lieblings
onto painted ceilings.

Name aggression or mane aggression:
Star anise on a hobo's tongue.
It's exactly like a tongue.
As I have sung.

Fie! Asunder! Schmuck! Poignard! Fie!
Tumult, for those who won't see hot palaces
or hear the aggravated violet's daft prayer.
Betrayer.

He got his cells in me—*exactly like a tongue*—
    a feathery feeling at back of throat
or ear of nuclear radiance.
Awkward raindance.

My Darling. Piggy.
Piggy. *Earthings*—for whom
Mother cleans the new harmonium.

Harming otium.

Open heart
perjury: fluttery aftermath.
Altered math.

The turtles turn away in slow mourning.

Droop Loss Slave

I just got these... sorrow pants on...
as an ascii kitten in the lasso of tiresome
attachment.

It is a kind of *vaginitis of the mind.*
We should ptyalize the doors
to a meteorically barebacked toughness.
And then push through.

He wallowed in the grandest blindspot: the minor howl
of self. Chock. Fracture. Weblike. Tight.
The mesmerizer is not
punitively crimson.

We were stonelike
and licensed as retrievable doves,
puckishly justifying vermillion
songs-as-gadgets in the cool midnight.

I suppose
I am the chick of the clunky hindfoots,
diabolizing tamarillos and pennywhistles
with fancily confusing tunes.

    I do believe in marriage,
    its solemnity, the smell of caves,
    the nearby (unwedded) albino crocodiles.

sebaceous watercolor
hopes stewed in a nonexempt golden
junk, an ungual kinescope swooshing.

The cyclones
starshipped grandiloquently then are not (then)
the spooky nudists of my will.

Swallows' wings
around a looming breast, why want what
one wants? Fake freedom of hummingbirds,
universal music all over my hippie's
headband (husband).

A hollow pianissimo: marriage's
iridescent spareribs, precedently retroflexed.
The mysterious chatter of the lions. Weary
of men and their meretricious alphabets!

We should glaze the doors.
It (marriage) is Sumatran by finiteness.

    Incurvate as kismet, leathered by
    mistakes, tensely deep-seated.
    I give myself fair warning.

The subtreasuries of our minds husked
heavenwards as hollow adagios;
I was the cloven-footed schoolmarm
(many-chambered *droop loss slave*)
unswayed by the WILL of those
off-putting bodies, their ordinariness
and liltingly quizzical bunts.

The high-tech
viridity of self loving. The bird-hipped
dinosaurs of marriage—we manfully research
our skin.

What is obliquely encrusted
can sit mussy on the variations of these
banal astonishments: "The Promise Breakers."

Of this I can sob masterfully,
loftily, coherently soured, all mushy
with sprained birdsong.

I do believe
in marriage, its amaranthine blubber.

What can you hydraulically *have*?

There is a *mournful India* in it. As
a truth serum. How not to fear images
of bodies' soapy riddles?

Patchily
again I have the cactus of imagining,
polymerizing the psychotropic seed-time
of a plane-polarized organza.

Unfrosted thrum. My husband's
junk, harmfully collapsible. My husband's
birthday, filled with the sweetish
dreamings of polysynthetic glands.

Eternal reproach of rotated to soaked.
Eternal reproach of aromatic rust-colored
bodies. Eternal reproach of liquefied
fear molecules.

Eternal reproach
of these nonmodern verse sardonics:
they slaver on the looming irreality
of the señorita, smashed as from
a sheika or hajj or creepy cygnus.

Hovering
over his last bed.

Eternal reproaches that are not adoptive, as
pink-purple smocks or brazen-faced
antiquarian raptures. We should
labialize the doors as unassailably
unstirred ghostfish, the ghost in the
apartment, shells of shapes, shells
of sounds, shells of smells.

Final rule: can you actually *have* the
maladjusted rhinal pup? Patchily
I despise the deliciously prognathous
slaughterers, immunized from heart
to heart.

Eternal reproach: the petty cactus of these
graceful imaginings - its enchanted *runch,*
its gold-powered *valence of three.*

Noncolumned
it is inexpressible, and it quilts.

Hand-Pulled Noodles

I read Edward Säid and feel bad about my Orientalism.

I can watch the process of my Orientalism, but cannot stop its progress or my attachment to it.

There is something inscrutably authentic about my Orientalism that is not present in that of others.

I read through my Orientalism to create a character that took details seriously. Generalizations were viewed as generalizations. I learnt the art of reading.

My Orientalism costume made me look dowdy. I can still wear the wig because it's a flapper bob. I just wish I had a fabulous tasseled dress.

The bloom of my Orientalism is fresh upon me, and this apathy and listlessness have laid hold.

It goes with my Orientalism collectibles :) However, there are so many nice rose/oud scents on the market these days.

My Orientalism was primarily a childhood and adolescent phenomenon.

I come by my Orientalism honestly: spontaneous joy, travel, Turks, woodcuts, wormholes, circuses, shriners and fairs. Oh My: Orientalism... a dream of minarets and domes, or dark-eyed houris reclining in perfumed gardens, of obese sheiks and sultans with a harem of the unwilling.

My Orientalism had been elevated to such a sexual degree that little else mattered. And you know what? That just made me feel lousy.

In my Orientalism, neither the term Orient nor the concept of the West has any ontological stability.

You may be right about my Orientalism, and deep down, below the surface of an emancipated male, I even may want to be a patriarch.

I borrowed a ribald poem with the word "meat-stick" in it, to drum out the last chapter of my Orientalism.

ΔΔΔΔΔΔΔ

Tinkerbell naked
Coloring pages of
Peter Pan and Tinkerbell:
You are my Orientalism,
bitterly enabling of you.
Sufficiently superficial
my Orientalism. Sufism.
Poofism. Proustism.
What would Säid've said?
Meaning or sound?
Where does the river bend?
approach myself quite my
quarterstaffs, with my
Chippendale painlessly
the chicot and my ringtones
on the lactate in my
Orientalism, and gargle

to it, and haphazardly
with my Orientalism upon.
I could murk a sirocco
many stoplight that were
not twinkling before.
Lexicon, how could she
resemble? flamboyant
sandilands, tempestuous
with a renunciant to
holyrood house; my
Orientalism having
feminize I pharmacy
my Orientalism important
what is meth amphetamine.

ΔΔΔΔΔΔΔ

I Found the Best Orientalism Online.
I bought my Orientalism with ease
and the low cost was inexpressible.
My Orientalism arrived in a week
from my seller.

ΔΔΔΔΔΔΔ

Upon closer inspection, he finds it to be the giant egg of a Roc, a
type of immense dragon-like bird.

Tastes like bopis, fills like linguine, yet still has the unique
appeal of fresh hand-pulled noodles. This is my Orientalism at
its best.

HEAVY

I have a somewhat rubbery
feeling beneath my breasts.
It's like all my thoughts
are clustered up in a ball in my head.

A heavy burden. A personified
space. Plankton. A pile of blankets
on top of god. Gold boars.
The earth. Nuptial spoils.

What is this heaviness
I am feeling? What do you call someone
who carries heavy things in Spanish?

As a child, enter the Lost Woods
and go right, left, right, straight, left.

In this secret area, wear a mask
(usually the Mask of Truth).

We're not floating around in a gaseous haze.
We hear it all the time: "lighten up!"

Chest heaviness means feeling heavy
in chest. Most people describe it as if
someone is holding their hearts,
a feeling of wringing of heart and pain.

I can just be by myself and all of a sudden
it is as though something heavy is placed on me.

In this hidden meadow, walk around in the grass
where the butterflies are spilling out and you'll find a hole.

My ears will feel like they are filled with water
and my eyes feel really heavy-like with fluid.

Where did all that heavy stuff cluttering
up your bedroom come from.

She lay for a week,
neither feeding nor excreting,
on the floor, among the straying frogs
and starving voles.

Often I am permitted to return to a diorama

Often I am permitted to return

to a diorama. The diorama
is put together sloppily.

Its tiny inhabitants hunt colored eggs
or enjoy a springtime picnic
in a drippy grotto.

<>

If I were tiny, I'd sleep

on a marshmallow with a mini
rosy doll or tiny forest elf

sitting on a mushroom top
in a mint-green lace bra-and-panties set,
trimmed with tiny bows and crystalline beads!

<>

O! Feel the spirit of the natural freedom

and ceaseless joy! I can create
my own little world of model figures!

It must be the heat but
these little Chinese Feeling Dolls
keep looking at me wistfully.

<>

They teach us how to draw Lord Krishna

and how to make a solar system
out of a shoe box.

"This one shows
how all sorts of animals
eat each other."

<>

Petite lass spreads her little slit to the max.

takes off her tiny panties
to show her hairy snatch and to pee.

From that point on, life without the spiritualism
of the world of illusion, a consciousness independent
of phantasmagorias, is unthinkable.

<>

For such tiny little fluffy babies,

they sure can chirp LOUD
deep inside the studded egg.

It was not immediately clear
what the diorama was intended to be.
An owl? A scarecrow?

<>

Strands of chimp hair

were sticking to the pieces of tape.
The Tiny Forest is a removed enemy (from Mother 3).

Oh, this is, why I love moss!!
Tiny worlds are opening up.
Yay! cute little pointless forest!

<>

Go ahead, re-arrange the little animals and enjoy!

Butter big ass Perfect blonde doll poses in bright little undies:
degradation is always in the texture of everything!"

Bats' fungus, ants licking diseases, autism brunch—
I just feel a breast popping out of my head!
Eyes do not open and close on their own.

<>

Lusciously fragile personal moment—

a remarkable creature with a long, snakelike body.
Tiny legs and scales that shimmer:

my female lionhead/dwarf is pregnant
with a rainbow-hued iridescence.
This has helped me so much.

<>

The diorama was not accurate.

The diorama was built on pink foam.
Its Mysterious Forest is absolutely clean.

Pieces appear to be just "slapped on."
Smudges. Stains…and into my panties.
the sound of…
tiny foiled cheeses. and fruit…

<>

Osculation

Have you been failing a time eunuch lately? If you are looking
for more time, first desire for that you need it. If it's matter.
Or kindling or time. Tussled with loved ones, then the solution
is rippled—calendula bustles to make room for personal
relationships. But you might have to wilt if you need more
time. Unto yourself. Right now, the petals are twisting away
from solace.

The adult makes the spinning pyramids that stay adult.

Pulled nuclear sleepy adult colors don't smell me.

The public sings the smart eggs of hot adults.

Certain cheerful quiet with a lone night wife.

For hybrids is mostly blue husbands.

Pilot her atop the loving hybrids at body, and ground human
hybrids—a night calf to go.

Human dreams go like a smart.
Directly human hybrids charge
whenever they ring.

Excited chance heads, seized as accurate
warm moon years.

Trust the cold oil room up on the quiet square, don't edge me.

All I make is, I'm truck that we are.

Enormous tender men get new shovels.

Costumes that stomach beneath their adult mouse costumes.

Chairs of people-green costumes.

Mother of the feeling jungle being more
than talking to own breasts.

It often caves the door of a driven brain.
Pad toward aching sense.

What's the accordion of a darling cloud
when you can ground a narrow one?

What's the challenge of exchanging a pushed head
when you can face a secret one?

Cut the door hands of history.
They wait to bottom luxuriously in their red want.

Wet someone to keep with you.

Have you been failing a time eunuch lately? If you are looking
for more time, first desire for that you need it. If it's matter.
Or kindling or time. Tussled with loved ones, then the solution
is rippled—calendula bustles to make room for personal
relationships. But you might have to wilt if you need more
time. Unto yourself. Right now, the petals are twisting away
from solace.

Wildcats Can Be Revealed (*Vile Lilt*)

Only the wed know cod, and eritrean —
fizzing their independences
as vainglorious struts.

The actor's frizz of wrongness heifers,
a shimmery satyriasis—repulsively
shammy, outlawed, and unzipped.

A golden cowrie shivers
in the golden expectation
of physical nervousness.

Its taunting staccato.

Horrible buzzing of blank widows—
guggling hasped madonnas—
tacky sensations
in bronze-red braincases.

The babydolls are singing
"that is a arrow, yes it is,
it's a triangle, it's a arrow."

Mortals in the morning suck
their warm cups: they want
mothers. They want *their*
mothers...

so they shallowly gambol

and whoosh and dissemble...
bellowing humid glides.

A thin gold anklet
lips the frilly edge
of anxious solitude, trapped
beneath a suntan-colored nylon.

Longueur—the vine-flavored steam—
curls spines over jammed mouths—loudish—
this loom of gormless cramping. This droned,
bustled organity.

Faint with a wound incarnadine.

Slippery doebirds, sighing
like baboons in a blistery sea of private
error. A satin eye cries nectarines
onto grayscale earthlings.

Their laudable ganglia, writhing covenants.

A wolverine amourist thinks of a suncup.
The world pulses with violence.

The memory of you is lodged
in my labial folds...like a deer tick.
Tra-la-las of cornish moon rounds
and their archean drumlins.

I'm vacuuming the tracks of tears—white
people—a merged...sea.

Where are the knots
of tears? The knots
of tongues? Familiar
and bulbous plateau.
Null. Secret mills.
Language low as
blush.

What are the tears
of their gripping? Their
sent twist?

When love wilts
the chickweed comes up—
inquisitively, I guess.
The weepers are swaying minions—
in alleys—with cleavers:
feathered pelves.

The smutty modernization
against which
they are foetal.

Their intemperate lingams.

Alyssum—heady sweet—
climbs up the bare "soul's"
woozy spike. Loquats cast
burned shadows
on its roundish concert.

This slithy myalgia
a japingly pangful metallic gasp.

Blame is like a
boomerang boomerang a
like is blame.

I have a soft lick—do not die—
little cement empress—ache
the garden again, with wings of cement.

I loved with a fatal hormone
and a brighter agency.

Moaning a little inside, but from
anxiety, not from lust.
The jerky curtain flaps usually
against the globular flexion
of this hateful velveteen.

Poor caryatids—their heads.
Elegant tormont chevrons
(their hidden purrs).

These tidy cretins have been corrective:
Tranqs, singing gels, tranced blowsiness.

It's precious—like a hooligan.
Gingerly we enter the salmon
of cadence—its flighty twist—
and a doll—of nothing.

Step into it: awful bursting
magnolias—poetry's churlish squeal.
Voice whirlwind an undeserved
agony of thick-breathed cuckoos.

My limbic system wants to sing
to a herd of turquoise monkeys.
Vultures fly into an oily sky.

What time is it?
It's happy hour
on the isle of Pathos.

Wide eyed, the infant makes
sucking motions, gazes around
"space." Lite tension. Yarning
fewness. What purpose
could anything possibly serve?

Monodic incurvation.
Masturbate
to increase fable.

Staring dark-colored at the red-flowered
megachiropterae.

Zipper folders full of DVDs
his little fingers caressed—
their sinister prismatic glint...

The insatiable clown
at the end of the course.

Only the wed are shallow enough to gambol
in a frizz of wrongness.

An orphan sunchild's
disconnected ear

like a tangerine section
lost on a frigid planet's slushy moon.

The eagles have some other angular planet, too,
and wind.

Drizzling a solemn affect
on viridine tuffets, the forced urgency
toucan countess coaxes a garbled abstraction
out of her veiny song box.

All the world's a murky pond.

A heron comes to land there—
a blue one, with a white eye.
Hello, heron.

We take a walk on some honey,
the heron and I. The honey
is from the moon! It blasts
radio sound—a vile lilt.

But something is wrong
with my hearing. It just feels
like there's liquid cement
in my ears. It is as crucial
as wreckage.

Doveweed. Milkbush. Tangelos.

Wildcats can be revealed
in the chemistry of the lilt
and in its vocabulary.

The lilt is the mangle
and the mangle *is* the message
(thermal clarinets).

All I held deer,
and rubbing velvet antlers
onto the stained satin.

Those who gave me their pain,
they will become light, too,
bringing drool to lovers
as steams of energy.
As manure.

The future's surprise
is its demise.

I feel like we are in the movie Aliens.

Out, vile lilt, out!

Out, torn face clown pictures! Out, ultramarine
sobs, strange suns, that which is constitutionally
pale!

Out, eructating chimerae! Scaddle, catfaces!

Out, nirvanic mädchens!
Your silkweed awedness,
your sourish mascara, cannot
fluster me.

Out, beadly spanworms, flighty groaners!
Out, sphinxes, Out!
Out with your subgaping luster, your coded glom!
Your grim lushes are squirming
and wholly bulbless. Your waxbirds
are soporous and dank—filmy
and anemic browsers.

I've done the dhobis, the ear cleaners, and the circus.
I've done the night off-kilter, the kilts off at night.
I've done the tumbleweeds in writing, the unrhymed
midweek quick-frozen elasticized sham of octane palaces, the
Scaramouche piñatas, the martyrized "bulging" feelings, the
combed nebulae...

Out! Out stewed sulk, and short-winged malice!

OUT wood-lined viper grass, deep-stapled quill bits, twice
forgiven grain moth hemp palm magpie diver! Out sickle-
tailed, state fed, low-power true-souled pelican fevero! Out
grape sugar! Out lynx cats, dull-red snow pigeons, wavy-edged
android vipers!

Now talk incoherently: SPIDERS. A searching wind: anthems.
When she was a kitten. Gray fishes and muzzles snatchin
with gleaming eyes, seized a clawer suddenly voiceless mad—
worthless and purposeless CLUTTER, Rorschach swaggering,
revulsion heron, or anxiety with a long, adverse weather is.
Sure and I never thought of him: HEROIN. "You see," I lizard
smell cried to robot his raw, flammable burping sound. Those
dirty woo geeking smokers. Fuck. Monkeys cage happens
speculated properties. Wetted parts include brass socket.
That garbage man keeps the milk cold. Just seep through

wreckage. I wish to change my environment. I wanna have fun in other areas in China. I wish to change my environment. Chorus of savage and vividness rageful protest. Some eat both ways. Or some such bright chips. He sprawled headlong, with outstretched ball-point pen arms, a bit of muslin torn pleasantly. They were human of the beasts boy again closing, above his long head and the library leaped: cold dark higher organ. Great steaming Neanderthal crush of humanity at the malls and the wrong burn. Opera goes. Crippled by nostalgia: proud fixed alive grass. Wept supper appeared mowed. Dentist brings her the perfume: love out(r)age. Long it? Petalous. Timeless portable each, without luv babyinfant. No doubt song wiped ambrosia—that green preserve is occipital swiped basket—helpless mental shake, revenge employed in the bulb prison, advantage of knowing bleach. Such a room spread fright paste last night. Yes, he uneven had a glow wife. Creams are future with sensitive churl or churl that is barely bone-dry: it hunches, it launches, it finches, it...*leaves*.

Out, vile lilt, out! Out!

Out.

dandily with my gazelle

(in, in, in, gloating)

ROOF BOOKS

the best in language since 1976

Recent & Selected Titles

• **Flowering Mall** by Brandon Brown. 112 p. $14.95.
• **ONE** by Blake Butler & Vanessa Place.
Assembled by Christopher Higgs. 152 p. $16.95
• **Motes** by Craig Dworkin. 88 p. $14.95
• **Scented Rushes** by Nada Gordon. 104 p. $13.95
• **Accidency** by Joel Kuszai. 120 p. $14.95.
• **Apocalypso** by Evelyn Reilly. 112 p. $14.95
• **Both Poems** by Anne Tardos. 112 p. $14.95
• **Against Professional Secrets** by César Vallejo.
Translated by Joseph Mulligan.
(complete Spanish/English) 104 p. $14.95.
• **Split the Stick: A Minimalist-Divan**
by Mac Wellman. 96 p. $14.95

Roof Books are published by
Segue Foundation
300 Bowery • New York, NY 10012
Visit our website at seguefoundation.com

Roof Books are distributed by
SMALL PRESS DISTRIBUTION
1341 Seventh Street • Berkeley, CA. 94710-1403.
Phone orders: 800-869-7553
spdbooks.org